Today is
FEBRUARY 3RD

Today is FEBRUARY 3RD

My Life with Type 1 Diabetes

MICHAEL MOORE

müllerhaus
[LEGACY]

TULSA

Today is February 3rd: My Life with Type 1 Diabetes
Michael Moore

Müllerhaus Publishing Arts, Inc.
DBA Müllerhaus Legacy
5200 South Yale Ave, Penthouse | Tulsa, Oklahoma 74135
www.MullerhausLegacy.com

Printed in the United States.

ISBN-13: 978-1-7328044-0-1
LCCN: 2018961764

Every effort has been made to trace the ownership of all copyrighted material
included in this publication. Any errors that may have occurred are inadvertent
and will be corrected in subsequent additions, provided notification is sent
to the publisher.

Cover and Interior Design by Laura Hyde | Müllerhaus Legacy
Edited by Christy Phillippe

A portion of all proceeds from
this book will be donated to **JDRF.**

If you would like to additionally support
JDRF's efforts to cure Type 1 Diabetes,
please visit **JDRF.org.**

Michael and Linda Moore
Photo credit: Mark Moore

There are definitely struggles with having T1 Diabetes. Some of those are physical, but some are emotional. One of those emotional struggles is how other people perceive our illness, especially in those important pre-teen and teen years. Everyone wants to be accepted, and included, and feel wanted. Sometimes kids are cruel, and they treat others that are not like them differently. T1 kids already have enough in their backpacks without having to worry about what other kids think about them!

I did wonder what girls thought about me being diabetic, and would that affect their thoughts about dating me, or even marrying me? I went out with this beautiful girl who worked with my mom. My mom had told her that I was a diabetic before we went out, so she knew. But she never looked at me like I was anything but me. She never was ashamed or embarrassed of me taking shots in public, or anything. But neither was I, and I told her that. She loved me for me and has done everything in our life together to encourage me to take care of myself the best that I could. She has rescued me from some serious lows, and is always by my side in my care. There is not another person in this world that I would want to share this journey with other than my wife, Linda! This book is dedicated to her, for her love and concern and care for me, and her love for her children, and her love for her family. Linda, this book is because you believed in me. I love you!!

Contents

Introduction

First of all, let me introduce myself to you. My name is Michael Moore, and no, I am not some famous filmmaker, nor am I a retired Major League Baseball pitcher. I'm just an average fifty-four-year-old guy, married to the most wonderful lady in the whole world, Linda. Together we have two children, Craig and Shelby. Today Craig is twenty-eight, he's married to Samantha, and they are expecting little Ryker in about five weeks. Shelby is twenty-five, and she is dating a really nice guy and working hard to make a living. I am not some famous athlete, I'm not a Hollywood actor, nor am I some multimillionaire who runs some major corporation. I am just a normal guy who gets up and goes to work five or six times a week, just trying to live the American dream and provide for my family. Linda does the same thing, working at least fifty hours a week at her own job. We are just normal, everyday people, trying to live life, provide for our family, and love our extended family.

But I want to share my usual-but-unusual story with you. I'm just an average guy—but I'm an average guy who shares a certain part of my life experience with millions of other people throughout the United States and around the world. This particular experience is also shared by many family members: moms and dads, brothers and sisters, grandparents, aunts, uncles, and cousins. The part of my experience that I am referring to is Type-1 diabetes.

T1 diabetes strikes not only young people, but people of almost any age. Many people are diagnosed at a younger age, with some children even being diagnosed in their first year or two of life. T1 can create devastating complications in the body, even leading to a very early death. T1 can affect a person's eyesight, nerves, kidneys, heart, and cardiovascular system. Poor control of one's blood sugar levels will hasten these complications, but good blood sugar control will delay these and even prevents certain complications from occurring.

My own family watched my mom's sister struggle with certain terrible effects of T1—and we attended her funeral in the summer of 1974. She was only forty-three years old. I was ten. Less than five years later, on February 3, 1979, I myself was diagnosed with T1 diabetes. I had hopes and dreams and a life to live, but now I was worried: Was my path in life to be blind by the age of twenty, or well on my way to an early death? I tried not to show it, but I was scared.

On the other hand, I loved competitive sports, so I think my attitude toward my T1 diagnosis sprang from my competitive nature. I decided that I was not going to let this get the best of me, that I would do whatever the doctors told me to do in order to take good care of myself. Now, I will be the very first to admit that I am far from perfect, that I have made many poor choices in self-care throughout my life, but I also was able to shake off those mistakes and stay determined to make the best of the life I had been given. There have been ups and downs, highs and lows (literally!), and good times and bad. I've always wanted to encourage others to do the very best that they can in managing their diabetes, but I really didn't know what to do. Every year I get sentimental around the date of my diagnosis, February 3. My wife's birthday is February 4, so I am always keenly aware of my emotions on these days, so happy to celebrate her birthday and enjoy her life, but keeping in mind the somber reality of the disease that could have already taken my own. It's definitely a reflective time, but it's also a time to thank God for bringing me this far. For the past few years, I've felt the need to share my story with others, so I started writing it down. It's actually taken me about five or six years to finish, because I would write mostly around that time of the year.

I hope that you find my story encouraging, and I hope that if you're living with T1 yourself, you will make the commitment to do your very best to manage this disease well, not just for yourself, but for the ones who love you!

Here is how my story begins.

– 1 –

My Dia-versary

Today is February 3. We all have dates in our lives that bring back memories and many different emotions. Birthdays, anniversaries, graduations—we remember each of these days every year. But every year as my wife's birthday rolls around, I also am very aware that February 3 is coming, and I begin to experience the many thoughts and emotions that go with it. Some things we go through in life will dramatically change things forever. On February 3, 1979, I was faced with that kind of life-altering, dramatic change in my life. I already knew the verdict before I arrived at the doctor appointment, but I still had hope that it could be something else, that it was not the same disease that had taken the life of my aunt just five short years earlier.

My aunt was only forty-three years old when she passed away from the devastating effects of diabetes mellitus, referred to then as juvenile diabetes. On that cold day in Oklahoma, I sat in the doctor's office and was given the same verdict. I was diagnosed with juvenile diabetes, and I faced the same life-altering change that she had been given—the disease that would challenge me like never before. I did like a challenge, though!

I had already been reading up on the disease. At that time, most of the literature and specialists in the field declared that this disease would more than likely shorten people's lives by at least 25 percent. That meant that I was likely going to be dead by the age of sixty. I sure didn't like that! My family had just buried my aunt at such an early age because of this very disease. I was sad—and I was scared!

My mother knew the pain of watching her sister go blind, the pain of watching her sister struggle with declining health, until she finally got that phone call from her brother-in-law that Rita had passed away. And now every emotion that my mom had felt about her sister and the disease that took her life was now focused on me, her son. She did not want the same fate to befall me!

There is no doubt in my mind that my mother begged God in heaven to take this disease away from me, but she also knew that it was my own fate to face. Thankfully, during that visit where I was diagnosed, my mom asked the doctor if I could still participate in sports. She knew how much sports and competition meant to me. And that day I also heard something that gave me hope. The doctor said that there had been a great deal of progress in managing this type of diabetes, and he thought that if I took proper care of myself, I could live a good life—and that included participating in sports. In fact, the physical activity would actually benefit me! He didn't have to tell me twice!

That day was a life-changing day, but it has since brought me to this day, almost forty years later, and my, how things have changed. But before I keep going, I want to tell you the story of my life, as far back as I can remember, and how it ultimately prepared me for that day…

DID YOU KNOW?

Type 1 diabetes is usually diagnosed in children and young adults and was previously known as juvenile diabetes. Only 5 percent of people with diabetes have this form of the disease.

In Type 1 diabetes, the body does not produce insulin. The body breaks down the sugars and starches you eat into a simple sugar called glucose, which it uses for energy. Insulin is a hormone that the body needs to get glucose from the bloodstream into the cells of the body. With the help of insulin therapy and other treatments, even young children today can learn to manage their condition and live long, healthy lives.

Michael, *three years and nine months*

– 2 –

My Earliest Memories

Even though I have roots that go extremely deep in Oklahoma, I wasn't actually born there. In the summer of 1963, my dad and mom packed up their belongings, along with their three children, and moved to Ashtabula, Ohio. I went along on that trip as well, safely tucked inside my mom's growing belly. My father had decided to move the family in order to take a better job and provide for this growing brood. I was born that November. Even though I might have gotten off to a start as a Buckeye, though, I can assure you that I am an Oklahoma Sooner through and through. (BOOMER!!!)

As a grown adult today, I can't even imagine packing up an expecting wife and three young kids and moving 1,200 miles away from any of your family members and all that you know. That had to be tough! But that is what you will see about my parents, that they had God, they had each other, they had their children, and my dad had a job that he knew would provide for our needs. My parents knew that because they had all of those things, they were truly blessed.

I don't have many memories of Ohio like my older brothers and sister do, as we moved away from there when I was five, but what I do remember

I hope will stay with me for the rest of my life. The town of Ashtabula sits right on the coast of Lake Erie in the northeastern part of the state. If you don't already know about lake effect snow, it wouldn't take you long to learn about it after moving to Ashtabula! We lived in a house on Eleanor Drive, and that house is where most of my memories of Ohio take place. The house was just blocks from Lakeshore Drive, which ran right by the lake.

One Sunday during wintertime, I knew we were supposed to go to church, but we weren't going. The snow was literally three feet deep, and I couldn't even go outside because the drifts were taller than my head! I remember looking out our front window and watching my brothers play in the snow. They were building tunnels through the powder; we could see them over by the driveway, then they would disappear, and they would show up by the front porch! It was crazy! I'm glad we moved, because I never have been as fond of winter as some people are. I am much more content when the weather is warm!

That being said, the summers in Ohio are when some of my best memories were made, memories that would shape me for a long time to come. My two older brothers both played summer league baseball, and of course my mom and dad took us all to the games. It was there that something grabbed my heart and my mind. It could have been the smell of the popcorn or the dry roasted peanuts, or seeing people eating the delicious fresh hot dogs, or smelling them smoking their cigarettes… (My, how times have changed!) It also could have been the cheers of the moms and the shouting of the dads, encouraging their sons to do the best they could—despite their coaches! The *crack* of the bat, outfielders scrambling to run down the ball, and people cheering the whole time—all of it was very exciting. But nothing was more thrilling to me than to watch a player run the bases. Whether he was flying down the first base line, trying to outrun a throw from an infielder, or stealing second base, it got something inside of me going. My ultimate thrill was to see a player rounding second base and steaming for third while the outfielder was fielding the ball and preparing to make a throw. The base runner was looking at the third base coach, who was waving him on, yelling, "Go, go, go!" Watching that player racing home to beat the throw from the outfield and knowing that both would arrive at the same time—I absolutely loved it. Then there was the slide into home plate right before the catcher could tag him, and the call from the umpire—"SAFE!" Some people in the crowd would be cheering and praising their kids, but there would also be those who were sad or upset at the outcome. While watching those competitions at such an early age to see which team would win, something came alive inside of me— my deeply competitive nature.

After each game was over, I would go out on the field, run up to home plate, pretend I hit the ball, and then take off running to first base. I would stop there but soon take off to second, and then my mind was completely in the game!

I would round second base and race for third, hearing the coach yelling in my mind, "Go, go, go!" Rounding third, I would race for home, knowing it would be a close call. I would slide into home, and of course I would always be safe!

I don't ever remember my mom and dad saying, "Don't get your clothes dirty," or "Stay off of the field," or anything like that. They might have looked at each other and said, "Oh no, there he goes again!" But I do remember my mom looking at me each time and asking with a smile on her face, "Were you safe?" That was all the encouragement I needed, that smile and the acknowledgment and approval of what I was doing. I was hooked!

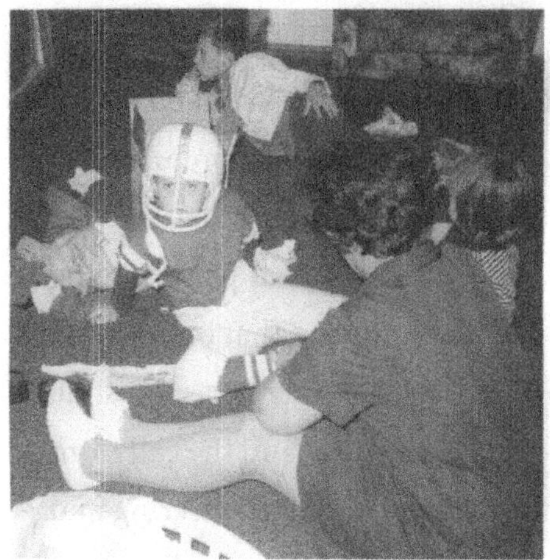

Left: Michael plays in his football uniform. *Right:* Michael celebrates his birthday with a cake and his mother, 1965.

I have other memories of good times in that house on Eleanor Drive. I remember climbing a big tree in the backyard, my first bee sting in the front yard, walking down the sidewalk after my first time out trick-or-treating, and more.

My mom used to plant a garden in the backyard, and one summer day I was out there with her while she worked. My brothers rode their bicycles over to the school, just a block or two away, and they were playing football there with some friends. As my mom was working away in the garden, we both heard my older brother, Mitchell, screaming. He was riding his bike down the street while holding one hand against his head. My mom ran over to him, and I followed close behind. He had blood flowing out from under his hand. My mom got to him and had him take his hand off of his head. That was my first time to see anything like that. Mitchell had fallen and hit his head against a brick wall. His head had been bashed wide open, and we had to take him to the hospital, where they put three stitches in his head to close up the wound. It was nothing major or life-threatening, but I'll never forget it. Mitchell was the same brother who first helped me put on a baseball glove, who started teaching me to play catch—something else that would impact me forever!

During our time spent living in Ohio, my mom not only gave birth to me, but she also gave birth to my younger sister in 1967. So then there were five of us, all of us Moores, and all of us MMs: Mark, Mitchell, Melanie, Michael, and Melissa. We would joke later in life that Mom was actually "Mom Moore" and Dad was "Master Moore," so we all were MMs.

In the summer of 1969, our dad gathered us around the kitchen table and announced that he had found a job back in Oklahoma, and that in thirty short days we would be moving back there. My older brothers and my older sister were ages six, five, and two respectively when they had moved to Ohio. Mark and Mitchell had memories of Oklahoma, but this would be new to the rest of us. A month later, we packed up and moved back to the oldest town in Oklahoma, Fort Gibson. I had fond but few memories of my time in Ohio, but a new life and many more memories were just waiting to be made!

DID YOU KNOW?

Emotional support, while not often initially considered, plays a key role in diabetes care. Kids with T1 who have a supportive and positive family structure around them will cope much better with the daily grind of counting carbohydrates, testing blood glucose multiple times each day, and dealing with the various highs and lows (both physical and emotional) of life with T1 diabetes.

Left to right: Michael, Melissa, Mitchell, Melanie, and Mark

– 3 –

Deep Oklahoma Roots

I mentioned earlier that my roots run deep in Oklahoma, and I would like to share a little bit of history about where I grew up. Fort Gibson was the farthest military outpost west of the Mississippi for a number of years. It was established in 1824 to keep the peace between the Osage Indians to the west and the Cherokee Indians, who were just arriving. After almost seventy years, in 1890, the U.S. military no longer needed the fort and it was abandoned.

Jeremiah Fisher married Catherine Smith that year in Fort Gibson. He had lived in Kentucky with his first wife, Mary Elizabeth, and they had two sons, Miles Edward and William. Unfortunately, Mary died at the young age of twenty-nine, and sometime before 1890, Jeremiah packed up his two young boys and moved west to Fort Gibson, where he met and married Catherine. Jeremiah and his sons farmed potatoes in the rich bottomlands of Fort Gibson, where the Arkansas, Neosho, and Verdigris Rivers meet. William, or Will, lived in a small house on the west side of town, close to the farmlands and only four or five blocks from the decommissioned fort. It was in that house in 1906 that my grandfather was born, and my mom was born in the same house much later, in 1937. When we moved back from

Ohio, my dad had an old house from the bottomlands moved and set right next door to that very house.

So you can definitely see that my roots run deep in Oklahoma, from almost twenty years before its statehood until 2017, from my great-great-grandfather Jeremiah, great-grandfather Will, my grandfather Ted Fisher, to my mom, who was born Virginia Lee Fisher!

At five years old, I don't remember worrying about moving to a new place. I think it is because we were moving back home, and the distance that my mom and dad had traveled away from home, that gap was now being closed. For my mom, getting to move back home into a house next door to her "daddy" was a great relief to her. (I can still remember her talking to my granddad and calling him "Daddy"!) And remember that garden that my mom was working in Ohio when my brother came home with his head split open? Well, I now knew where she got her love of gardening. My granddad had a beautiful garden, and we all enjoyed his fresh vegetables. I have so many fond memories of seeing him work so hard in that garden!

One other ironic thing really topped off this move back home. My dad's family had lived in a couple of different places around Fort Gibson, but they eventually settled in a house on the west side of town, catty-corner to the same house where my mom was born. Mom and Dad had lived across the street from each other, become high school sweethearts, married right out of high school, had five children, and then moved them all back home to live next door and across the street from their grandparents! I don't think it could have gotten any better than that!

I never knew my dad's dad, as he passed away when my dad was just sixteen. But we had Granny Moore, and we had Granddad and Nanny— we were truly home!

In Fort Gibson, we lived a block away from the church we attended, and my mom and dad made sure that we were there every time the doors were open. That is where I made my first friends, and some of those were kin to me—imagine that! Our house was also only four blocks away from downtown, and we walked there many, many times, not knowing then about the rich history that surrounded it. But there was one other thing that was in close proximity to our house: About a block away was the town baseball field, and from that summer until my senior year in high school, all of the baseball that was played in our town took place on that field. I was too young to play when we first moved back to Oklahoma, but I will tell you that if there were ball games being played, no matter what age, my granddad and nanny were there, and so were we, chasing foul balls, eating popcorn and corndogs and candy, and watching all the kids play ball. That was the small hometown life that we lived, and I loved it!

DID YOU KNOW?

Despite all of the corndogs and candy that I ate at those games, **nutrition is one of the most important pieces in the puzzle of learning to live well with T1 diabetes.** Understanding how different foods affect your blood glucose and learning to develop solid meal plans will be a crucial part of your daily routine—and help you to live your life to the fullest!

Michael (middle row, first on the left) and his peewee baseball team sponsored by Carl's Jewelers. Sammie, Michael's dad, is in the back row, second from the left.

$$- 4 -$$

Time to Play!

Like I said, when we moved back, I was too young to play organized ball. At that time, unlike now, you had to be eight years of age to join a team. But that didn't stop me from being out on the field when games *weren't* being played, nor did it stop me from perfecting my skills in our yard with my dad and my brothers and sisters. Even at the tender age of seven, there was no doubt in my mind that I was ready to compete. None!

When I learned that tryouts were about to be held, I told my mom that I wanted to go. She knew what would happen, but she let me go anyway. I headed out onto the field with guys who were a grade ahead of me, but not only did I hold my own, I was as good as any of their best! I was so excited!

But then it came time to give our birth certificates to the coach so he could verify our ages and eligibility. The coach was Mr. O'Dell, and he was also the elementary school principal. He looked at my birth certificate, then looked at me and said, "Son, I really would love to have you on my team, but the rules say you have to be at least eight years old. I'm sorry, but you're not going to be able to play this year."

I was devastated! I started the long block-and-a-half walk home. When I finally made it there, I sat down on the old wooden steps going up to our front porch, my glove still on. I hung my head and cried for a bit. My mom came out the front door. She had known all along how old I had to be to play, but still she asked me, "How did you do?"

I looked up and, with sadness and some anger and frustration, told her that I wasn't old enough to play.

She looked at me and said, "But how did you do?"

All of a sudden, my sadness was gone, and I looked up and told her that I thought I had done great, and that I could have played better than a lot of the older boys!

She said, "Well, you just keep practicing, and you'll be ready for next year!"

That was all I needed to take my mind off of my disappointment and start looking forward to playing the next year.

Fast-forward one year. Do you remember how I used to run the bases after my brother's ball games? Well, that practice came in handy. My first time at bat in uniform, playing in the Peewee C league, was amazing. I stepped up to the plate and slapped the first pitch thrown to me out to left field—and ended up with a triple! Heaven, I was in heaven! Those same older boys whom I couldn't play with and the guys my age won a summer league minor league state championship about eight years later!

As I grew in size and skill, there was this one huge constant in my life, and not just in mine, but also in the lives of my brothers and sisters. That constant was the fact that no matter what we were participating in, no matter what, my parents were always there to support us.

Baseball was, of course, the first organized sport in which I was able to participate, and from Peewee C baseball, which I entered at eight years old, to American Legion baseball when I was eighteen, my mom was our official scorekeeper and my dad always helped coach. Even in high school, where someone from the school was the official scorekeeper, my mom would still have her scorebook with her at every game, and she would diligently score the game like she always had done.

I played one year of junior college baseball, and although the team traveled quite a bit, if there was a home game and my parents could get there, they were there. They would drag along their lawn chairs and jackets and whatever else they needed, but when my mom opened her lawn chair, there it always was…her scorebook! I might not have always appreciated my parents' support like I should have, but I will tell you this: It was the most impactful thing on my life, period, and that is the real story of my life!

DID YOU KNOW?

Exercise is also a key component of a happy and healthy life with T1 diabetes. Along with all of the other benefits you will receive from being active, your diabetes will also respond in kind with more stable blood glucose levels. So stay motivated and get out there and exercise!

Despite his diagnosis, Michael was an active athlete and loved to play football.

My True Love...Football!

Baseball was the first sport I could participate in, but it wasn't the sport that I really loved. My true love was football, and growing up in Oklahoma in the 1970s, I quickly learned that in the fall, there was only one type of football that you paid attention to: OU football!

I realized even at an early age that I was fairly quick on my feet and that I had really good balance and excellent hand-eye coordination. With those abilities, there was only one position that I wanted to play, and that was a halfback in the devastating wishbone formation. My dream was to someday play for the OU Sooners, and look at the talent that I idolized: Joe Washington, Greg Pruitt, and Billy Simms are just a few of the great running backs whom I watched whenever I could.

One year during football season, my Nanny Fisher had fallen at the county courthouse while serving on jury duty, and she broke her hip. She was mending well, but she still needed a walker to get around. Not long after, we were watching the OU-Nebraska game next door at their house. The game was being played in Lincoln, Nebraska; OU was behind, and it was getting late in the game. OU ran a flea-flicker, and Elvis Peacock took the ball over fifty yards down to the 2 yard line. We were all jumping up and down, cheering, and when we looked over, there was Nanny, jumping up and down and cheering, leaning on her one good hip! That's a fan right there!

Back then there were no youth football leagues. We had to wait until we were in the seventh grade to be able to put on pads and start hitting each other. I had a good first year as a young running back, which only made my dream of playing at OU even stronger. OU football coach Barry Switzer actually came to Fort Gibson when I was in eighth grade to visit with one of the seniors about playing at OU. As he was walking down the hallway with one of our coaches, I called out and told him to come back in four years to watch me! That was as close as I ever got to playing at OU, but I don't think the dream inside of me ever died.

I wasn't a big kid, but I was quick and agile, and for high school football back then, that was a great advantage. I didn't like to lift weights that much, but I did enjoy anything that would improve my quickness, balance, and leg strength. During the summer, even though it might have been the season for summer league baseball, I still liked to go up to the high school football field and run bleachers, sprints, and agility drills. If there was someone there to throw the ball around with or practice kicking with, I was all-in. I was learning to push myself and trying to excel at being an athlete. Whatever the sport—football, basketball, baseball, or track and field—if it was happening, I was there.

And as usual, during all of these things going on in my young sports career, my mom and dad were there every step of the way!

In August 1978, I started the ninth grade. Putting in extra workouts and training had really started to make a difference. I was now almost five-foot-eight, and I weighed 142 pounds. I was looking forward to this football season; I could hardly wait. For all of the excitement, the season came and went with little fanfare, but I still had a good time learning and honing my skills. I scored a few touchdowns and started breaking longer runs. I was happy.

When football season ended, of course we went straight to the gym to start basketball practice on November 1. I dug right in, and soon we had a pretty good basketball team. All was good in my life, and I didn't have a worry in the world.

When I was younger, I rarely got sick, but in December of that year, I got the flu, and it kept me out of school for almost a week. That case of the flu really kicked my butt. I had received quite a few "zero absences" certificates in grade school, so it was unusual for me to get that sick for that length of time. It happened at the end of the semester, and I had to complete some of my homework at home to keep up. But I eventually got over it, and soon Christmas break began. I was looking forward to getting back to school and playing more basketball!

DID YOU KNOW?

I was a kid who loved sports, but even moderate levels of exercise when you are dealing with T1 diabetes require a bit of care and vigilance. **It is very important to maintain the proper balance of insulin doses with the food that you eat and the activity that you do—even if it is as simple as house or yard work.** Planning ahead and knowing your body's typical blood glucose response to exercise can help you keep your levels from going too high or too low.

After going blind due to diabetes,
Michael's Aunt Rita relearned to type
so she could return to working.

– 6 –

My Mom's Sister

I'm going to backtrack here a bit. I have mentioned my mom's sister, my aunt Rita. After we moved back to Oklahoma from Ohio, I actually got to know her. She and her husband, Eulle, would visit Nanny and Granddad frequently, and of course we would visit with them as much as we could.

Aunt Rita didn't have any kids of her own, so she loved on us as much as she could. She was also blind, so she never got to actually see us, but she would sure touch our faces and love on us all the time. She was fairly brittle, and she took her time as she walked along, usually with someone leading her. I remember well a leather-bound box that she always had with her. She kept all of her medications in it, which was quite a bit. She also kept syringes in that box, and she would have to take shots. I didn't pay that much attention to her health issues because I was usually outside playing.

In the summer of 1974, Mom and Dad loaded us kids up, and we went to Rita's house for the weekend. It was a little unusual for us to go visit over there, because there was literally nothing for us kids to do, no one to play with, but we were there for almost two days. We wondered what our parents were thinking, but as I look back now, I wish that, as a ten-year-old, I would have loved on Aunt Rita that entire weekend.

We finally returned home, but the very next day, I remember so well, our phone rang. It was Eulle, we learned, when my mom answered the phone. My parents did not show sadness very much throughout my childhood. They showed their smiles and their laughter and love, but I don't remember ever seeing my mom cry—up until this particular day. As she was talking, she began to cry as Eulle told her that Rita had passed away peacefully in her sleep the night before.

My mom's sister Rita was gone far too early, at the young age of forty-three. My mom fell to the floor weeping at the loss of her sister. I didn't know how to process it all. When my mom got off the phone, she had the terrible job of going next door and telling her own mom and dad that their other daughter had just passed away.

I remember the funeral, and going to the cemetery, and visiting with other family members during that time. I'm sure it had been talked about, but I hadn't really known what was wrong with Aunt Rita other than that she had been in poor health. If only I had known—but at ten years old, I didn't understand life and death enough to make the right choices. If I had known that five years later, I would be dealt the same hand that had shortened Aunt Rita's life on this earth, I sure would have loved on her any chance I got, and that weekend I would have spent the whole time visiting with her. To this very day, I feel a strong sense of connection to her. I often feel like she is watching over me from heaven.

DID YOU KNOW?

Families are extremely important when T1 diabetes is diagnosed. This is a disease that affects the whole family. Whether you are a parent, sibling, or family member of someone who is suffering from T1, your support and understanding can make all the difference!

– 7 –

Classic Symptoms

Let's return to January 1979—and basketball season. I was in the ninth grade, and my older sister, Melanie, was in the eleventh grade. If I wasn't playing a game but the high school was, we would both be there. Whether it was at home or away, we were there.

But then, on a weeknight in January, someone noticed something about me and said something that made me start to think. I had been feeling unusually tired lately, but I thought it was just from getting over the bad case of the flu that I'd had in December and the constant busyness and hectic nature of my life.

One of my very best friends at that time (and to this day) was Kevin Perry. His dad, Carl, owned a jewelry store in Muskogee. Carl was an avid Sooner fan and an all-around sports fan. From the first year that I played organized baseball through the summer after I graduated high school, I played for Carl's Jewelers. Carl would spare nothing for our young careers. Whatever we thought that we needed, he would get for us. This man and his son, Kevin, were truly loved by my family.

It was Carl who noticed something wrong about me. Carl took Kevin and me to a high school basketball game in a nearby town. On the way home, we stopped at an Arby's restaurant to get something to eat. And, of course, Carl paid for mine, like I was his own son. What he noticed, however, was that as soon as the cashier put my drink down on the counter, not only did I pick it up and take a drink, I gulped down the entire thing, then asked for more.

Carl said, "My, you're thirsty!" And I replied, "I'm *always* thirsty!"

At that moment I realized that something was going wrong in my body. And as time progressed, I became more and more tired all of the time. As you now know, if there was a sporting event going on at school, I was determined to be there. One day after school in late January of that year, I came home and lay down on the living room floor to go to sleep. I told my dad to wake me up at 6:30 so that I could go to a wrestling match. He tried to at that time, but there was no waking me up. My body was just too exhausted.

By 1979, both of my brothers were living out of my parents' house. Only me and my older and younger sister were left at home. One Saturday morning during that January, my mom saw what should have been clear all along. We lived with modest means, and that meant we had only one bathroom in our house. Crazy, right?!

On that morning, I had just gone to the bathroom. But not long after that, my mom noticed that I was back knocking on the bathroom door, telling one of my sisters to hurry up and get out. My mom looked at me and commented, "You just went to the bathroom." That's when I told her, "I go to the bathroom all the time!" I used to jog home from school, and I told her that I couldn't even do that anymore, because I always needed to pee so badly before I got home.

By the time I got out of the bathroom that day, she had retrieved *Better Homes and Gardens Family Medical Guide* and opened it to the chapter about the endocrine system. She had it turned to the disease called "Diabetes Mellitus" and asked me to read it. When I read through it, I looked at my mom and said, "That's me."

I probably should have been in the hospital right then, but not knowing for sure whether I actually had the disease, Mom called the Children's Clinic of Muskogee and made an appointment for the next week: on February 3.

The following week was terrible, as my health deteriorated so quickly. I went to a high school basketball game later in the week and didn't get home until late. But when I tried to lie down in my bed to get some sleep, I just couldn't. I was extremely thirsty, and my body felt burning hot. I grabbed a sheet off of my bed and went into the living room to lie down on the couch. As I lay there, hot, sweaty, and terribly restless, I still could not get to sleep.

I finally got up to go to the bathroom. In the one small bathroom in our house, the bathtub was right next to the toilet. We didn't have a shower in there until the following year, so we always took baths. To help us rinse off or rinse our hair, there was a two-quart plastic pitcher always resting on the side of the bathtub.

When I went in there late that night, I was so tired that I just sat on the toilet to urinate. As I sat there, so hot and so thirsty, I looked over at that pitcher. When I finished going to the bathroom, I leaned over and grabbed the pitcher, turned the cold water on, and filled it up. I started drinking it, and I did not stop—I could not stop—drinking. I finished drinking two quarts of water at one time, and then I turned around to the toilet and threw it all right back up. It felt so good, and it did seem to cool me down a little. So I filled up the pitcher again and slowly drank about half of it. I held it down. Then I went back to the couch, lay back down, and finally fell asleep.

Unbelievably I still was able to get up and go to school the next day, and I remember thinking about going to the doctor and what he might say. I probably knew deep down what the diagnosis would be, but I was still hoping it would be something simple.

DID YOU KNOW?

A diagnosis of Type 1 diabetes means that your pancreas is no longer capable of producing insulin. Through multiple daily injections with insulin pens or syringes or an insulin pump, it will be up to you to monitor your blood glucose levels and appropriately administer your insulin. You will need to work closely with your healthcare team to determine which insulin is best for you and your body to manage all of the symptoms that T1 diabetes can bring.

– 8 –

February 3, 1979

We got up that Saturday morning and got ready to go the doctor. I wish my dad was still alive to ask his perspective, but all I remember is me and my mom going. My dad might have been there, too, because my sisters were plenty old enough to be home alone, but I just remember my mom during the visit. This could be because, if you remember, it was her sister who had died just five years earlier—and this day would forever forge a bond between my mom, her sister, and me.

I have looked back on this date every year, and I wish so much that I could tell my aunt Rita how I am doing and what is going on in my life. I have always felt that she is watching over me from heaven, and in 2011, my mom went on up to heaven to help her, because watching over me is not always a one-person job!

The Children's Clinic of Muskogee was a fifteen- to twenty-minute drive from our house. I know Mom and I talked a little about diabetes on the way, but I really didn't want to know anything about it at that point. I felt like I was in a fog on the drive there, and in my heart, I was wishing that the doctor would tell me, us, that I had something completely different. Something other than a disease that I now understood had taken the life of my aunt when she was just forty-three years old. Something other than a disease that I had read could shorten my life by 25 percent. Anything else!

I do remember well that when we got there, it was cold and cloudy. We got out of the car, and I woke up out of the fog that I had been in. I knew that now it was time to find out what was wrong with me. Even knowing deep down what was probably coming, at least I had hope that I would feel better if I could get some answers. I didn't really think about what my mom might have been feeling, but I knew this: She was there by my side, right there to take care of me.

We went inside and got checked in. Remember, I had hardly gotten sick at all when I was younger, but I had been to this clinic before. The mom of one of my best friends had worked here as a nurse—and she had recently passed away from breast cancer. Other than that, I had only seen the doctor that she had worked for a time or two, when Mom had taken my sisters there.

We now sat in the exam room full of toys and children's books, watching as a few other moms brought in their coughing and snotty-nosed kids. My name was finally called. It was time to get this over with.

The nurse took us back into the exam room and did all of the normal things, weighed me and took all of my vital signs. Remember that during football season, just six months before, I had weighed in at 142 pounds? Well, at that appointment my mom and I realized just how much weight I had lost. I now weighed just 120 pounds! I really had not realized that I'd lost that much weight. When the doctor finally came in and did his checkup, he listened to my heart and lungs and did a visual checkup. He then said they needed to check my blood sugar. So Mom and I went over to the lab area, and at this point I can now say, "I'm SO glad time and technology have changed!" I hated that V-shaped lancet that the nurse drove right into my finger!

After that painful experience, we went back to the exam room and waited for what seemed like hours. These days, we are impatient when we have to wait five whole seconds for a blood glucose reading! Anyway, the doctor finally came in and asked us to step into his office. We sat down, and then, without beating around the bush, he said, "Well, we checked his blood sugar, and it was 474, which means he definitely has diabetes."

I hung my head down and cried, but the doctor kept talking. He told us that I needed to check into the hospital immediately, where they would start giving me insulin and teach me all that I needed to know about how to take care of myself. I looked at my mom, and remembered that the last time I'd seen her cry was when her sister had died, but there she was, wiping away tears.

It was February 3, a day that would impact my life forever. But what that day was not, it was *not* a day of doom and gloom, or a day of worry or of death. Even though those thoughts have come and gone during the years, what my mom and dad and family did for me over the next few years would shape the way I feel about the hand that I was dealt. For that reason, I share this experience with you today. My life had changed, but none of us were going to let it slow me down!

DID YOU KNOW?

After the initial shock of a diabetes diagnosis wears off, your family will begin adjusting to life with diabetes. **With a little planning and preparation, you can resume all of your normal day-to-day activities, such as exercising or going out to eat.** Diabetes should not keep any child from achieving their highest goals. Remember: there are Olympic athletes, professional football players, congressmen, actors, and rock stars who all live with diabetes!

– 9 –

Getting Started

On to the hospital we went, checking in, being admitted to a room, putting on that awful gown, and of course, receiving my first injection of insulin. The doctor had also ordered a chest X-ray, and an absolutely beautiful technician came to take me to have this procedure done. She wheeled me to the X-ray department, and when we got there, she asked me to stand up facing the machine. I followed her instructions, and she told me to put my arms around the machine and roll my shoulders around it as best I could.

I don't know if it was the insulin or the dehydration, but whatever it was hit me right then. I turned around, looked right in this gorgeous lady's eyes, and watched her come straight for me. I put my arms out toward her, and she wrapped her arms around me. (It sounds really good, doesn't it?) But I was out! Passed out smooth!

The technician actually kept me from hitting the ground, and the next thing I knew, I was waking up in a wheelchair. I had never passed out before, and I sure didn't know what to think. She got me back to the room and helped me settle back in bed to rest.

This reprieve was only for a bit, though, as the nurses and dietitians all came in to teach me what I now needed to know. My mom learned everything right along with me, as things had changed a great deal from when she had watched her sister cope with diabetes. I practiced giving injections on an orange until I felt ready to give one to myself; I learned all about blood sugar control and diet, and the complications this disease could pose to me. It all seemed easy enough.

A girl my age was in the room next to me, and we became friends. Giving myself my first injection was a breeze, as my new friend was right there to watch, so I had to be brave, right? Actually, I did just fine, and today, thousands upon thousands of injections later, I still do just fine.

I learned that first night that I hadn't passed out earlier that day from low blood sugar. Back then, I loved to watch the original *Star Trek*. It came on at 10:30 at night, and I would stay up later than my mom liked me to so I could watch it. That night, on the first night of this new journey, with my mom in the recliner beside my bed, we sat and watched TV. We watched the news at 10, and at 10:30, *Star Trek* came on.

Everything that I had gone through was catching up to me at this point. I had been receiving insulin in my body for several hours, which was giving fuel back to my cells and putting fluids back in my body, so I was tired, but in a good way. I was also relieved to know that there wasn't a question anymore about what was wrong. I now knew that this was my life.

A minute or two after *Star Trek* came on, I closed my eyes and fell asleep. At 11:00, just thirty minutes later, I was awakened by the worst jittery, shaky feeling I had ever had. My mom was reading quietly next to me, and as soon as I jumped, she looked at me and asked me what was wrong. I was drenched in sweat, and I told her I didn't know.

She called the nurses immediately, and I have to admit, at that moment I was scared. The nurses got there and gave me some orange juice. They reassured us that my blood sugar had just dropped too low, and that those were the symptoms. As my sugar rose, I finally started getting drowsy again, and I went back to sleep. I think I had an eventful enough day that first day!

I spent the next few days getting adjusted to the new changes in my lifestyle. We had been told that I might be in the hospital for up to a week to get my system regulated and to gain confidence in what I needed to do. I thought, *A week? No way! I have a basketball game on Thursday night, and I'm not going to miss it, period!* When my mom told the doctor how I felt about missing the game, he promised he would see how I did and make a decision in a few days. I checked into the hospital on Saturday, February 3, and I left the hospital on the following Wednesday morning, just in time to get back to my life of sports.

DID YOU KNOW?

I traveled away from home quite a bit for sports events. If you or your child goes on a trip, here is a helpful packing list of things you will need to bring along.

- Insulin
- Syringes
- Blood glucose testing supplies
- Pump and/or continuous glucose monitor (if needed)
- Ketone testing strips
- Glucagon
- Glucose tablets or fast-acting sugar to treat low blood glucose
- Medical ID card (*a child should always wear a medical ID bracelet*)
- Day and night phone numbers for your physicians and health-care team
- Emergency contact numbers
- Batteries
- Snacks like peanut butter and crackers
- First aid kit

Michael, #32, plays with his ninth-grade basketball team against their rival, Haskell, days after his diagnosis and leaving the hospital.

– 10 –

The Beginning and What It Held for Me

When we got home from the hospital, I got dressed and went straight to school. I wanted to make sure that they wouldn't keep me out of the basketball game because I had missed too much school, so I made sure I got to school before lunch that day.

Going back to school was a little weird, as some friends welcomed me and asked me how I was feeling, but some weren't sure what to say. But I was still the same person that I had been just four days earlier, only with a few changes in my lifestyle. I have never hidden my disease or been ashamed of it. There is absolutely nothing to be ashamed of, nor to hide.

Since the day I was diagnosed, I have always told people about the warning signs of low blood sugar, just to be on the safe side. But all I was really concerned about was how this was going to affect my ability to play sports. I was feeling so much better, and I thought that this disease couldn't affect me all that much—but watching what it had done to my aunt at such a young age made me worry just a bit. I wanted to prove to myself that I could do whatever I wanted to do. And it was time to find out.

That Thursday night we traveled out of town for a ball game, and of course, my mom and dad were there for that game, too. It was probably more nerve-racking for them than I knew, but they didn't show it. I, on the other hand, just wanted to get back to playing ball. I was extremely disappointed when my coach told me I was not going to start, since he wasn't sure I was ready. He knew that I thought that I was, and I let him know that.

I did get to play in the game, though, and it was uneventful. I made a couple of mistakes and missed a couple of passes. When the coach asked me if my vision was okay, I told him it was a little blurry. Not too much was made of it, and I left that game a little upset and wondering about my future. Remember, I had just left the hospital the day before. As the rest of the week went on, I was back in school and back to practice. My blurry vision cleared up quickly, my strength and my quickness were back, and I was back to practicing as a starter.

Our next basketball game was to be an afternoon game at home, and I knew that I was going to get to start. The cool thing about this game was that when there was an afternoon game during the school week, the entire school body was let out to come watch. On this day we were playing against the team from Haskell, Oklahoma. We had played against these guys not only through the seventh, eighth, and now the ninth grade, but since we had been eight years old in baseball. We had developed a great rivalry with the guys from Haskell, and they had a great team. There would be no better test for me to prove to myself that everything was going to be alright—but I was nervous.

That afternoon soon arrived, and we were all out on the floor, warming up in front of not just the normal crowd filled with our parents, but the entire school, as well. The game got going, and I was feeling fine, actually really good, but I wanted to make an impact. Our point guard brought the ball down the floor, and he passed it to me on the left side. I made one stutter step to the baseline but then drove to the middle of the lane and went in for a layup over their center and scored! Man, I was on fire at that time. I ended that game with 12 or so points and a steal or two. On this day I knew that everything was going to be fine. I knew that there were going to be challenges, but I was not going to let this disease keep me from living my life.

My mom came up and told me I'd played a great game and that she was very proud of me. I didn't know until years later what that game did for my mom, and in fact, it wasn't until after she passed away in 2011 from the devastating effects of Alzheimer's that I would find out.

DID YOU KNOW?

It can be hard to go back to school after a diagnosis. If your child is nervous in the face of uncertainty, here are some tips for you as a parent to help them tell their friends about their new experience:

- Understand that being diagnosed with diabetes is a life-changing event. For many kids, it takes time to accept their new reality and be ready to share with others.
- As a parent, you may have the urge to tell everyone you know that your child has diabetes in an effort to ensure their safety, especially at school. Though your school nurse, teachers, and principal need to know, it's really up to your child to tell their friends and anyone else they want to know.
- Before spreading the news, ask your child how they feel. If they aren't ready to share, then respect their decision and help them to feel more comfortable about diabetes.
- However, if they are ready, talk about ways to tell others, including their friends. Remember to keep explanations simple and direct and prepare them for some of the reactions they might face.

Michael in his NSU football uniform.

$$- 11 -$$

High School and Beyond

I went on to play three years of high school football and baseball, two years of basketball, and to compete in track and field when I had extra time. I tell you all of this not because I was some outstanding athlete, but because I want you to know the deep love that I had for sports and competition. I went on to set a few records in football, and one that we thought was a record until someone produced a newspaper clipping from the late 1960s showing what he had done that proved that my "record" wasn't accurate. I still think I had a great game anyway. My junior year I played in a game where I scored five touchdowns, and I kicked four extra points and a field goal. I'll take that as a great memory!

In baseball, remember when I told you about my first at-bat in PeeWee C, and that I hit a triple and I was off to the races? Well, my senior year in baseball, I had a pretty memorable game. Our new high school baseball field had been under construction my junior year, but it was ready to play on for my senior year. I was the leadoff hitter, so I got the great honor of being the first Fort Gibson player to ever hit on that field.

As I stepped up to the plate, I dug myself in and got ready. The first pitch was on the way, and I sent it deep over the centerfield fence. *Boom!* My first pitch was a homerun! My next at-bat was just the same, only over the left field fence, on the first pitch. And guess what, on the third pitch thrown to me, I drove over the right field wall. Three at-bats, three pitches thrown to me, and all three were homeruns. Needless to say, my next at-bat they did not throw anything for me to hit and they walked me. I think that was a great way to break in that new ballfield!

I have always said that I didn't turn my diabetes into an excuse for anything. But as I look back now, I realize that I just wasn't prepared to be on my own as I went to college. I went to a local junior college on a baseball scholarship. The fall schedule was okay, and I was doing pretty well at taking care of myself. But as spring rolled around, it became a much tougher schedule.

We would go on the road for sometimes days at a time, mostly having only fast food to eat, but we would occasionally eat cafeteria food. At that time, I was taking regular and NPH insulin. I rarely checked my urine for sugar, just going on how I felt. I know, I know, that wasn't good for me, but it was what it was.

It was tough to play at full capacity when you spent hours in a van, didn't eat very well, and most likely had a blood sugar level that was too high. On spring break, we actually got to fly to Arizona and spend the week playing against numerous junior colleges there. I finished the week playing at Arizona State University. It was a great week—but very tiring.

At the end of this week, my mom called me at the hotel and told me some sad news. Carl Perry, the man who had given us all that we had ever asked for while we had played on his team, had passed away from cancer. Also at the end of this week, I decided that baseball was not for me, and I left the team. I was relieved, knowing that I would not have to travel so much, and I actually started to feel better.

That summer I went and talked to the coaches at Northeastern State University about walking on and playing football there. They said that I was welcome to walk on, and so that's what I did. I only got to play on the scout team offense as a running back and a receiver, but I enjoyed it. Practicing, weight lifting, and a much more regular schedule really helped me to regain my health. I actually started to gain some weight, getting up to around 170 pounds.

It was also here in my second year of college that I let myself get into the party scene way too much. I let my grades slip, and I ended up having to quit the football team. I know that kids will be kids, but if there is one thing that I regret, it would be letting myself drift into the party scene and let myself down. I ended my college education with almost 100 credit hours but a long way from a degree.

DID YOU KNOW?

T1 and partying do not go together well! Here are some tips to help you and your teenager with Type 1 diabetes prepare for situations when they might be offered alcohol, cigarettes, or drugs. These tips will also be helpful as your child transitions into adulthood, when it becomes legal for them to drink at the age of 21, or if they are frequently around others who do (for example, at college).

- Ask your diabetes care team to discuss with your teenager the effects of alcohol, cigarettes, and drugs on diabetes.
- Follow up with your teenager about their conversation with the diabetes care team. Be sure they understand what can happen when a person with diabetes drinks alcohol, or uses tobacco or drugs.
- Discuss peer pressure. Share ways you handled these kinds of issues when you were their age.
- Listen closely and try not to nag.
- Remind your teenager to always have their diabetes supplies with them and to wear a medical ID bracelet or necklace.

Linda Moore
Photo credit: Mark Moore
July 17, 1987
Mike and Linda
before they
were married.

– 12 –

God's Gift to Me

It was the spring of 1986, and I was attempting to keep my education going, but I was really just keeping the party going. I knew I wouldn't be able to go back to college in the fall, and I needed to start working.

A friend and I started doing lawn work, and in late March, we dropped in to my mom's workplace to see if we could take care of her office's lawn and landscaping. We didn't get the job, as they already had someone else doing it, but I got something even better.

As I talked to my mom in the back hallway of that office, a young lady walked around the corner and said, "Excuse me," as she passed. When she walked on down the hallway, I told my mom to let her know that I wanted to go out with her.

My mom soon called me and gave me the young lady's phone number. Mom said that she would go out with me if I called. On April 12, I went out on a date with Linda Niedermayer, a quiet young woman who seemed very unsure of what to say. I, on the other hand, always had something to say, and that must have been what set her at ease, because we were able to talk easily. It wasn't long before we knew that we were very serious about each other, and we spent every free moment together that summer.

When August rolled around, my friends started heading back to NSU, and the guys I had played with on the football team were showing up to start practice. I had such strong ties with these guys, and I really wanted to be over there. I found out that on the Saturday before they were supposed to report for practice, there was to be a big party. I just had to go and be a part of that.

I took Linda over to a playground that was near her house, and I made a really terrible mistake. I told her that I thought we might be getting too serious, and that I was going to spend the weekend thinking about it. She was heartbroken, and I was so stupid!

I went to Tahlequah on Saturday morning, to where the party was soon due to start. We started drinking early, and it wasn't long before the party was on. Late in the day, I thought I was feeling spunky, so I started messing with the starting center for NSU. Remember, I was five-foot-nine and 170 pounds, and he was around six-foot-two and 230 pounds. We were outside on a gravel driveway, and I started trying to wrestle around with him. What was I thinking?

I went in for his legs, believing I was small enough to get under him and get to them, but no. He just picked me up, turned me upside down, and drove me into the gravel face first. I had a nasty little gash on my nose and blood all over my face. I cleaned it up a little but kept right on with the partying into the night. I was trying not to think about what I had told Linda and how she must have felt, and I thought that if I just kept on drinking, it would go away.

I finally passed out at this guy's house late that night. I woke up with a terrible headache very early in the morning, and all I could think was, *What have I done? Did I really break a beautiful young lady's heart, all for some party?* I did, and all I wanted to do was get back to her and tell her how very sorry I was—and to tell her that I never wanted to be apart again.

I headed back to her house in Muskogee and got there around 10 a.m. I rang the doorbell, and her mom answered the door. I asked if Linda was there. At that moment, Linda came around the corner and walked over to the door. Her mom turned around and walked away, shaking her head. I had an open gash on my nose and dried blood all over my face. Linda asked me what had happened, and I told her about the party. She looked as if she had been crying, but she said, "Let's get you cleaned up."

I grabbed her hand and asked if she had been crying. She said yes, that she had been crying ever since I'd told her what I'd said on the playground. I looked at her and told her that I had made a terrible mistake, that I did not want to leave her ever again, and that I truly loved her.

She forgave my stupidity and got me all cleaned and bandaged up. I had just about blown the greatest thing that God had given to me, placing this beautiful, loving, caring lady in my life. In December of 1986, I asked her to marry me, and on July 17, 1987, we started our life together.

Linda was very happy to join my family, as she would later tell me. Her mom and dad had divorced when she was thirteen or so, and her sister was seven years older than she was. It was just Linda and her mom living together. Linda was quiet, and she felt as if she didn't have much of a family life.

At work, before she ever met me, she would listen to my mom talk about her family and what her five kids were doing. She would long for the type of family that my mom was talking about. She had all of these feelings, not knowing that soon she would be joining that very family! So she did not just love me with all of her heart, but she also loved my mom and dad so very much for the type of parents that they were. She was very happy to join us, and as I write this, we will be celebrating our thirtieth wedding anniversary this year!

Linda Moore has been an inspiration to me. She is the hardest worker that I know. She has been a great mother to our two children, Craig and

Shelby. She has been by my side through thick and thin. She has never been demanding or pushy when it comes to my health, but she is always encouraging and always by my side. She has brought me back from more than one very low blood sugar event, and I would tell her that she is my angel, sent here to earth just for me! I truly am blessed to have her as my wife, and our two kids and now a daughter-in-law, Sam, are all such a blessing, as well!

DID YOU KNOW?

Dating for the person with T1 diabetes can be a bit tricky. It's ok if you keep your diagnosis private at first. Just be sure to wear a diabetes medical ID and consider the following questions prior to leaving for your date:

- How will you handle dosing for a meal or snack?
- What snacks will you bring and how will you carry them around?
- Will you be too anxious about how you're going to manage your diabetes to have a good time?
- What if you are going on a date that involves some form of physical activity? Are you okay with checking your glucose levels around your date?
- How would you handle a serious high or low?

Here are some tips for sharing your diagnosis with your date, if you need to:

- Keep it quick and simple, like, "I have diabetes, so I have to plan a little when I eat. I keep track of my blood glucose levels."
- Remember that most people are very caring and concerned, and sometimes curious, too.
- Be ready to answer a lot of questions about diabetes if you bring it up. But that can be a good sign—it could mean a second date is in your future!

– 13 –

My Mom's Book

If only one good thing comes out of me writing this book, I hope that it helps those who are living with or love people who have diabetes. I especially hope that I can encourage parents of children with T1, that I can guide them and challenge them to fight for their kids with all that they have.

Parents, learn not to push your child with T1, but gently nudge them in the right direction. Don't demand, but encourage, and through all the ups and downs that will come, remember that it is not you who has the disease. No matter how much you might want to help, it isn't your life, and ultimately it's not your decision. Demanding, pushing, arguing, and fighting will not bring your child's diabetes under control. It will usually result in just the opposite: a child who resents their disease and doesn't accept it, which leads to poor control and poor results. If you, the parent, demonstrates acceptance of what's given to us in life, and if you encourage your child to be the best that they can be in whatever they do, you will give them the courage and the strength to live a long, healthy life.

Most importantly, never stop showing your love for your kids. Be there for them, and show them what love is—that it is an action and not a feeling. There is nothing greater that you can do for your child than to love them and let them love you in return!

Another reason that I have shared my life story is to encourage those with Type 1 to live their lives to the absolute fullest. The more you learn about your disease, the better equipped you will be to handle all of life's challenges—and there will be many if you have this illness! Dealing with Type 1 is a challenge in and of itself, but the most important thing that you need to watch is your *attitude*!

Left: Michael's parents, Ginger and Sammie

Below: Michael's mother at a baseball team celebration.

What you think in your head when not another soul is around—that is what will usually dictate your life. Are you telling yourself that you now have a disease that can get really bad, and that you know your life will never reach its full potential? Do you say to yourself that you will never develop the lifelong friendships that you could have developed because of your "problem"? Do you ignore what your doctor tells you to do?

If so, I'm here to tell you that this is what will kill you. Instead of thinking these things, I want to encourage you to think a different way. Tell your beautiful self that, in spite of having a disease that can bring complications to your life, you are going to do everything in your power to take care of your health. Wake up every day knowing that you *can* handle what's been given to you. Realize that you can be happy and enjoy all of the things that you have been blessed with. Determine in your mind that you are *not* going to let this slow you down, and know that if you take good care of yourself, you will not be slowed down. Most importantly, don't push away those who love you. Your emotions may get raw sometimes, especially when you're not feeling well, and those emotions could lead you to take actions that push people away. Resist those urges. Instead, let people love you and show you their concern, especially your mom and dad!

I've mentioned how my parents loved my siblings and me. They took us to church and taught us about God. They encouraged us to do the very best that we could in school. They taught us how to respect and care about other people, and they showed us what love really is: giving your time, energy, and life to someone else.

When Linda and I started dating, I realized how much my parents loved all of us. She noticed that we didn't tell each other the words, "I love you." And I noticed that every time we left *her* house, *her* mom would tell her that she loved her—every time. As Linda and I grew closer, she asked me, "Why do you and your family seem so close, but I never hear you tell each other the words 'I love you'? I hear my mom tell me those words all the time, even though I feel so far away from her."

I looked at Linda and said, "I know that my parents love me by how they are and what they do, not what they say!"

I know this is what made Linda love me and my entire family so much. But it was also around this time that my family finally broke the ice and started telling each other that we loved each other, too!

In my later teen years, I remember my mom saying that she was going to write a book about her experience with diabetes and how it had affected her. That was all she said, but I think I remember her doing a little writing now and then. I never saw a completed manuscript, though. Then I went off to college, got married, and had children. Nieces and nephews and cousins came along, our family grew, and my mom became "Nanny" to all of us.

Around her seventieth birthday, we all started noticing that she was acting different, frequently at a loss for words. When we confronted my dad about it, he actually broke down in tears, He told us that she was getting very forgetful, but she was too stubborn to go to the doctor. He promised that he would get her to go, and he did, but this was the beginning of the downhill journey for my mom. She would live only four more years, and on November 16, 2011, our beloved Nanny was gone. Remarkably, my dad cared for her at home himself until she was gone, another act of selfless love shown to his grown children.

A few months after she had passed away, we were all at Dad's place when he said he had something for me. He went over to a desk, grabbed an old envelope, and came over and handed it to me. Puzzled, I asked what it was.

My sister said, "You remember when Mom said she was going to write a book? Well, that was the beginning of it."

I was a little stunned, because I had already forgotten about it, but I was also emotional, knowing that I would get to read her thoughts about my disease. I could not read it there in front of them, so I took the envelope home.

I told Linda that I wanted to read Mom's writing by myself, and she understood, so I took it into our bathroom, closed the door, and opened the envelope. I unfolded three notebook pages, recognizing my mom's handwriting instantly. That alone was touching enough, to see something that she had written some thirty years before, but the emotions came flooding in as I began to read her words and feel her emotions about events that we had shared many years before. And as I read, I realized that her thoughts and feelings were eerily similar to the things that I felt and the thoughts that I had at that time—only they had been written from her perspective.

That's another reason for me to write this book, to share the thoughts and feelings of a parent of a child with T1 diabetes, the thoughts that Mom never got to share. And here they are.

From my mom:

Less than four months ago, my husband and I heard the doctor say, "Your son definitely has diabetes!" So few words, and yet what an impact I felt from them. Only five years before, my forty-three-year-old sister was buried after diabetes had ravaged her body. She was nine when the doctors discovered she was diabetic, lost her sight completely at age nineteen, married at twenty-five (having never seen her husband), became pregnant and was forced, by her physical condition, to have an abortion, and then continued to experience almost every problem that a diabetic is prone to have. In spite of all this, she remained a good-natured, warm, loving Christian lady. She was an inspiration to all who knew her.

But now diabetes had struck even closer. My son! My fifteen-year-old son who is active, intelligent, handsome, and who dreams constantly of being a professional athlete. I know the impact I felt was magnified many times inside him when he heard the doctor's verdict. As I looked at him, his head was bowed and tears were streaming down his cheeks. My heart ached for him as only a mother's heart can ache. If I could only take his place, but there was no way.

The first question that was asked of the doctor was how this would affect his sports life. The doctor assured him that he could participate in the sports that he had been involved in, which included football, baseball, basketball, and track. But, first, a stay in the hospital was necessary to stabilize his condition. He had lost about twenty pounds, as he was receiving no nourishment from the food he ate. Glucose cannot enter the body's cells and nourish them without the help of insulin, which a juvenile diabetic does not produce.

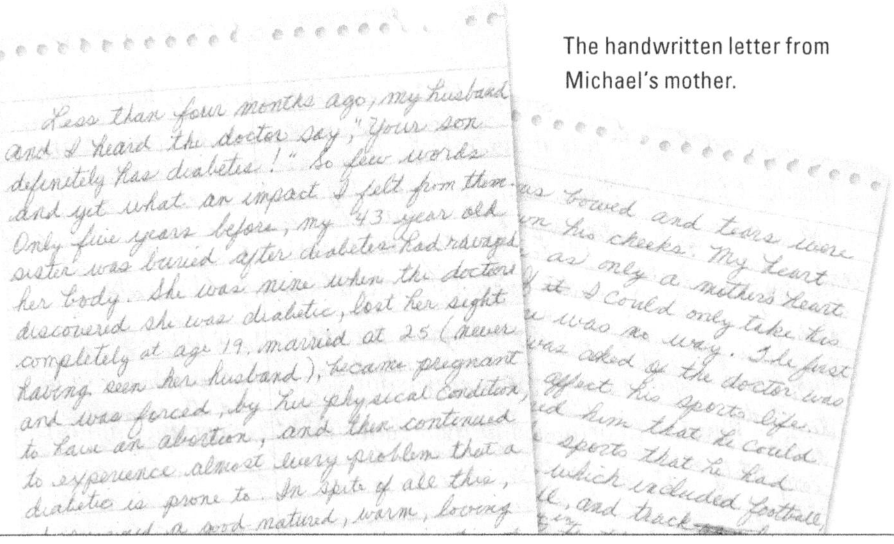

The handwritten letter from Michael's mother.

The other symptoms he experienced were excessive thirst, frequent urination, and blurry vision. The doctor said he could be hospitalized for a week, but he checked in on Saturday morning and was discharged on the following Wednesday morning. His complete lifestyle was changed in four days.

A diabetic must follow a very regular schedule. Two shots of insulin (which he gives himself), four urine tests, meals in about the same quantity and about the same time each day.

A short time after being released from the hospital, he got the opportunity to see how he could function on the basketball court with his new constant companion, diabetes. The junior high basketball season was drawing to a close, with only two games left. He had started every game for the FGJH except for the one game that had been played while he was hospitalized. This was an out-of-town game and he played, but not too well.

The final game of the season came a few days later on the home court with arch-rival Haskell. It was an afternoon game, and students were dismissed from class to attend the game. Michael had an excellent game—the best he'd ever played. He was extremely aggressive on both offense and defense, and he scored 12 points to help FG gain the victory. More than an FG victory was evident that day. Michael had scored a victory for himself. He knew he could make it, even with diabetes.

Life has changed for Michael, but when he saw that he could adapt to the changes, he has begun to do very well. I'm sure he will have periods when he's "down," but he has enough faith, courage, and strength to bring himself back up. And he's learning all he can about diabetes—he must know all he can to fight it. And he, his parents, and all who know him, I'm sure, are praying for the day when there will be a cure for diabetes.

Those were the words that my mom had written—about me! I love her, and I miss her and my dad so very much!

DID YOU KNOW?

If you are the parent of a child who has just been diagnosed with T1 diabetes, during the years ahead, you'll experience many of the same growing pains every parent faces as their child matures and gains independence. But you will have an additional transition to make—helping your child learn to manage diabetes. Your family has its own way of communicating and working together to solve problems and face everyday challenges. After a child's diabetes diagnosis, it's more important than ever to talk with each other, even when it hurts, even when it's challenging, and even when it's difficult. It will bring you through the tough times and help your child live their greatest and best life.

– 14 –

*Thirty-Eight Years Later—
and Still Counting!*

Although my mom laid her pen down many years ago, those four pages in her handwriting have meant so much to me. To read in her words the worry that she had, and the fear that I might meet the same fate as her sister did, is very touching. And, of course, I had those same concerns and feelings myself.

It is now February 2017, and the T1 world has changed drastically since then. Insulin pumps, blood glucose meters, extremely fast-acting insulin, and even continuous blood glucose monitors are now available to most patients. Diabetes researchers have been ferocious in their search not only for a cure, but also to improve the care for patients.

Not long after I was diagnosed, my mom got involved in the Muskogee County JDF. I wish now that I had started earlier to support this organization, but as an active teenager, I thought that I had better things to do. Mom and I went to some meetings together, and we participated in a couple of fund-raisers, but that was about all that I did back then.

I really don't remember how long Mom participated in the JDF. But I hope now that in sharing my story, I can do my part in supporting what is now called the Juvenile Diabetes Research Foundation. Research is costly, and the JDRF has funded over 2 billion dollars of research, many of their funds coming from donations. Their vision is a world without Type1 Diabetes, but until that goal is accomplished, there will always be a need to fund their research. I hope that after hearing my story that you will choose to support this wonderful organization.

If you looked at me today, you would probably have no idea that I have T1 Diabetes. I have gained a little too much weight the last few years (something I am working on), but other than that, I look like any other fifty-three-year-old man. Sometimes people think that T1 is not that bad, that I just take insulin and check my sugar and all is well. I can tell you it is not that simple. I thank my God in heaven that He has made me able to handle the demands this disease puts on my body and my mind. Some people are not able to handle these things, and their bodies succumb to its effects. I want to share a little story about this that forever will be with me.

I was diagnosed on February 3, 1979, and in August of that year, I started playing high school football. The *Muskogee Phoenix* was our local newspaper, and we read it daily. Besides three television stations, that was how we got our news.

A lifestyle reporter wrote a story about children with diabetes, and I was asked to be in the story, along with a young lady from Muskogee. Julie Morris was a senior at Muskogee High School who loved playing the piano. It was a great article about the advancements that had been made in diabetes care, and how we were participating in sports after we were diagnosed. They had pictures of us, and mine was absolutely terrible! But it was still a great article. I had met Julie and her mom before, but that was about all of the contact I had with her.

Later in my life, I managed a Tex-Mex restaurant in Muskogee. Linda and I were married, we had both of our children, and I was doing fine with my health. I enjoyed seeing people I knew in the restaurant, as well as meeting new people.

Late in the 1990s, the store had been remodeled, and it had become a very busy restaurant. I began to notice a certain customer come in regularly, an older lady who would bring her daughter in to get the same thing every time, two soft chicken tacos. Her daughter was almost completely blind, and the mother would lead her over to the counter, where they would order their food to go.

I would typically ask how they were, the mom would chat with me, they would get her food and then leave. It became a habit, as they would usually come in on Mondays, Wednesdays, and Fridays. I had no idea who they were. Then suddenly they stopped coming in. I thought that perhaps they were upset with our service or our food, that we had done something to offend them. But after a couple of months, I saw the mom pull up in the parking lot and get out alone to come inside.

When she came over to the counter, I asked her where her daughter was. We were standing just across the front counter from each other when she looked at me and choked back tears. "She passed away."

I looked at her and began to piece things together. I knew that her daughter was not much older than I was, but she had looked very unhealthy. Her mom told me that her daughter had been on dialysis, and each time when she finished, she would want soft tacos. I commented that her daughter was awfully young to be on dialysis and asked if she was a diabetic.

When she said yes, I finally asked the name of her daughter. She said, "Julie." In a stunned voice, I quickly asked, "Julie Morris?" The mother acknowledged that it was the girl who had been featured in the newspaper article with me years before.

I cried with her and told her how sorry I was. I asked her if she knew who I was, and she said she did. All that time of them coming in to eat, I had no idea

Muskogee youths coping

By BARBARA BASHORE
Assistant City Editor/Lifestyle

"I would rather not tell anybody I'm a diabetic . . . I don't like people feeling sorry for me," says Julie Morris, 17.

The attractive Muskogee High School senior shrugged, then turned to the affirmative nods of two other young people sitting in a semi-circle.

Despite their reluctance to talk about themselves, the three agreed it was important that they tell how they are coping with juvenile diabetes. Julie, Mike Moore, 15, and LaDonna Arnett, 8, all have the disease. A fourth youngster, Matt Staggs, 11, of Muskogee, came in to tell his story later.

Juvenile diabetes is not just for kids. It strikes teen-agers and young adults as well. And all of them have one thing in common: they must take daily injections of insulin to stay alive.

With juvenile diabetes, the severest form of diabetes mellitus, the body loses its ability to manufacture and/or utilize insulin— a chemical necessary for the assimilation of carbohydrates. Without it, the body cannot convert these sugars and starches into needed energy.

Symptoms of diabetes can include increased thirst, increased urination, weight loss in the face of increased appetite, itching of the skin, frequent tiredness, vision changes, slow healing of cuts and bruises.

The only known treatment for juvenile diabetes at this time is a combination of insulin therapy, diet and exercise.

The cause and prevention of diabetes are still unknown. At present, it can only be treated, not cured. For this reason, the Juvenile Diabetes Foundation, a nationally-accredited voluntary health agency, has as its primary objective the support and funding of research to find a cure for the complications and, ultimately for the disease itself.

With this in mind, a Juvenile Diabetes Foundation fashion benefit will be presented at 7:30 p.m. Saturday in the Muskogee Fine Arts Auditorium. Titled, "Joyful December Fantasies," the style show will feature Miss Oklahoma Jill Elmore as emcee, a teen disco modeling number, the newest in winter fashions from J. C. Penney's, and door prizes.

Tickets are $2.50 for adults and $1.25 for children under 18, with all proceeds going to the foundation. Tickets are available at Penney's in Curt's Mall and may be bought at the door.

A little more than 50 years ago, diabetes was a dreaded disorder that doomed the patient to a life of misery and an early death. Then, in 1921, came the discovery of insulin, and the diabetic's prospects improved dramatically.

Now, with the modern knowledge of treatment, the average newly-discovered diabetic eats well, works and plays normally, and can look forward to a long and productive life.

Julie's parents, Mr. and Mrs. Batie Morris Jr., southwest of the city, discovered she had diabetes at the age of 8. She learned how to give herself insulin injections by practicing on an orange. Since she must have two injections each day, Julie sometimes finds herself using a needle at school.

"It bothers other people watch-

Julie Morris

Matt Staggs

Mike Moore

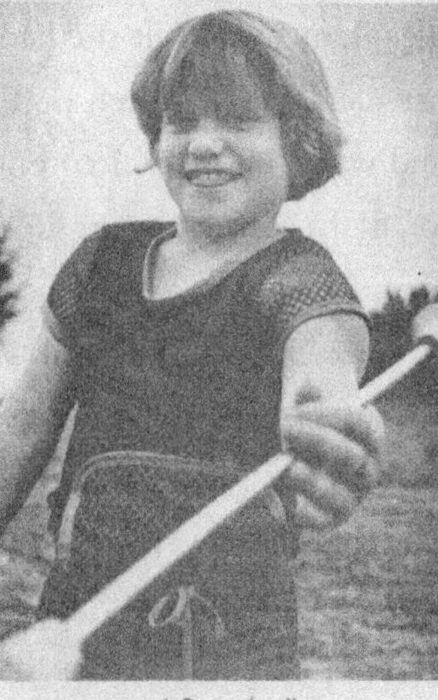

LaDonna Arnett

with juvenile diabetes

ing me more than it bothers me," she says, smiling. "I told my close friends they should learn how to give injections."

Mike, son of Mr. and Mrs. Sammie Moore of Fort Gibson, learned only last February that he was a diabetic.

"Last football season I weighed quite a bit, but then, this year, I started losing weight. I used the bathroom all the time, craved sweets, and was always thirsty and hungry. I lost a lot of weight and was tired all the time. Then one day I went to the doctor, and we found out what it was," he says.

What was his reaction when he learned that he had diabetes?

"I was kind of sad at first . . . but I was more scared than anything," Mike recalls.

"The first time I gave myself a shot, it took me three or four times to get the needle in right. I'd stick it in a little bit, then pull it out and try again. Then,

---

Photos By Ron Tarver

the next time I tried it, there was a girl in my hospital room watching me, so I did it the first time. She later became my girlfriend for a while."

LaDonna, daughter of Mr. and Mrs. James Arnett of Fort Gibson, was only 17 months old when her parents learned of her illness. Requiring insulin injections for six and a-half years, the small blonde girl has been giving her own shots since she was 5.

"I give myself shots in the thighs and stomach; my mother gives them to me in the arms and hips," LaDonna says matter-of-factly.

Since she has lived with diabetes virtually all of her life, the daily routine of injections before breakfast and again before supper is just that to LaDonna—a routine. Friends who know of her illness accept it and treat her just like any other kid.

Matt, son of Mr. and Mrs. Ross Staggs, 2839 Skyview Ave., has been using insulin since he was 3. He remembers that he used to "eat candy a lot," but other than that, he doesn't recall too much about the time his illness was discovered.

Although he learned how to give himself shots at a camp for diabetics in Texas, Matt says he doesn't do it unless there's nobody else to do it for him.

About the only thing he can't do because of diabetes is eat pies

or cakes. He is very active in golf and tennis, and is making quite a name for himself on the stage.

He has been in three plays to date: "Gypsy," "Flowers For Algeron" and was young Will Rogers in the Tsa-La-Gi production of "The Cherokee Kid."

"My friends treat me just like anybody else," Matt says, grinning. "The only thing is when they eat cake or something for snack, they know I'm not supposed to . . . so they offer me something else."

Is it hard, watching other people eat all the sweets he likes so well?

"If they offer it to me, I can say no. But if it's just sitting there, I'll take it anyway," he says sheepishly.

Having to watch his diet bothers Matt more than anything about having diabetes—including injections.

A happy, active young man, he likes geography at school and enjoys playing the trumpet, on which he says he is "so-so. But I'm good for my age."

Mike also understands the importance of a balanced diet, although he admits to sometimes "slipping." He just received his driver's permit and learned he is restricted to having food, fruit or candy within his reach while driving. A physical examination every two years is also required to keep the license.

What is the hardest thing to adjust to as a diabetic?

"I can't eat pecan pie, and I can't go barefooted (because of poor circulation in the feet)," says Mike.

"I can't think of anything," Julie declares, " . . . unless it's that I don't like people feeling sorry for me when they hear I have diabetes."

"There's nothing I can't do except eat sweets," says LaDonna.

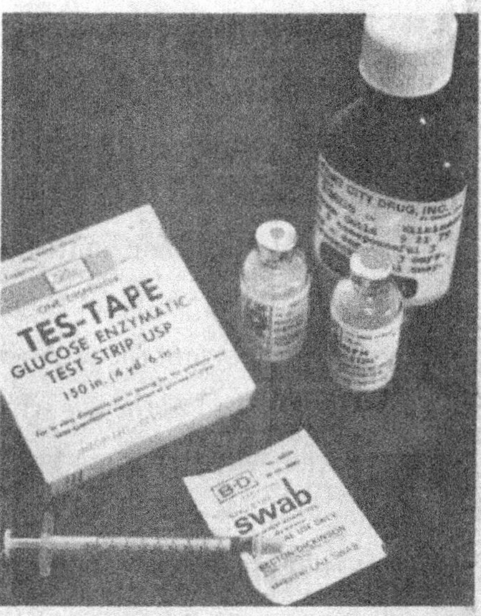

TWO THINGS a person who has juvenile diabetes must do every day are take insulin injections and test his urine.

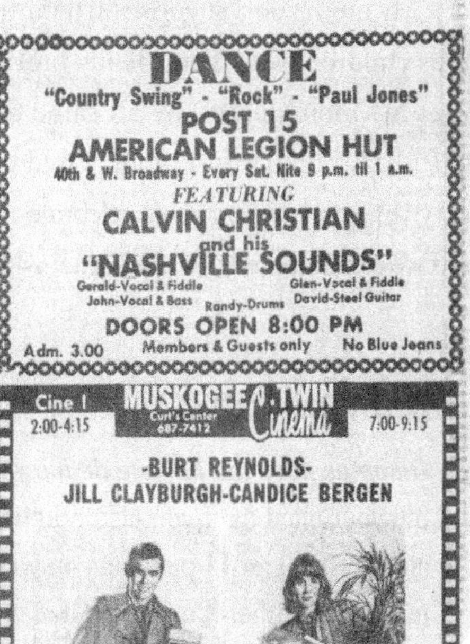

who they were. I hadn't even thought about Julie Morris in twenty years, and of course she didn't look healthy, which really changes you. I was thirty-five or thirty-six, and she was probably thirty-seven or thirty-eight when she died.

I went home that night and cried when I told Linda about what happened. That is way too young to be taken from your loved ones, and I was so very thankful for my relatively good health.

I was also closing in on a little milestone that had been stuck in my head since that Saturday morning in 1979 when I had been diagnosed. The older I grew, the more important the number *forty-three* became to me. It had always been stuck in my head as the age when my aunt died, forty-three. Sometimes I would question whether or not I would make it to the age of forty-three, and how my life would be. Would I go blind and have to have my wife lead me around? Would I not be able to walk very well because I couldn't feel my feet? These questions were not anything that caused me real trouble or worry, but they were rolling around in the back of my mind.

My mom had a surprise birthday party for her seventieth birthday. All five of us children were there, as my brother and his wife flew in from California. After my mom's party, we all came to my house and celebrated my birthday, which was number forty-four. I told everyone how I had felt about the age of forty-three, so that year we celebrated that I was healthy and as ornery as ever, and we remembered our aunt Rita, who had been taken from us far too soon!

DID YOU KNOW?

Diabetes does not have to define your life! You can achieve anything you put your mind to, if you also practice healthy self-care and manage your illness. Don't let T1 put limits on your life. Take charge of your illness and manage it, rather than letting it manage you.

– 15 –

Here I Come, Fifty-Four!

I have always wanted to share my life with others who have Type 1, but it has taken me a while to put all of this down on paper. Writing about my life and my illness has taken me on an emotional roller coaster.

My mom started showing symptoms of Alzheimer's disease in 2007, and she passed away on November 16, 2011. She had just turned seventy-four. My dad took care of her throughout the entire downhill journey, showing his never-ending, unconditional love for her. Only four years later, on November 7, 2015, he joined her at the throne of God. All of this having taken place in November makes my birthday even more reflective. As I am writing this, it is October 2017. On November 11, I will turn fifty-four. And next February, in 2018, will be my thirty-ninth T1 anniversary. I plan on being a little somber and very reflective of God's blessings in my life. I will be grateful to celebrate my wife's birthday the next day, as we do every year. I will have a three-month doctor appointment around the middle of that month, and I will be looking to turn in good numbers to my endocrinologist. It will also be time to plant onions in my garden! All of that is just to tell you that I plan on living my life and doing what I love—and so should you!

I do want to finish up by talking directly to those who have been diagnosed with T1. Until those research scientists who are so diligently searching for a cure can reverse what has happened to us, it is really up to each one of us to make good choices and take care of ourselves the best that we can.

As you have learned about me, I am willing to admit that I have made some terrible choices. I would encourage anyone in their high school and college years to avoid the party life the best they can. I've read stories from parents who talk about their son or daughter with T1 who went off to college and refused to accept the challenge to take care of themselves—and they ended up in the hospital in a diabetic coma. Or I hear about T1 adults who will not check their sugars and do not take their medication. This is insane!

I hear so many people with T1 complain about having to get their blood work done so often. But the A1C test is the very test that gives your doctor the information that he needs to help you adjust your insulin levels and your diet. Just recently, my blood pressure had gone up substantially. I was given a diuretic to add to the blood pressure medication that I already took. My body did not like that at all! It did help with my blood pressure some, but it made me feel terrible—and it drove my sugars up. How do I know this? Because I check my blood sugar regularly! And if I'm feeling bad or out of sorts, I might check my sugar twice the number of times as I do on a normal day. And then I adjust my insulin accordingly. (Please talk to your doctor before doing this.)

I quit taking the diuretic and was given more of my regular blood pressure medication, and that brought my pressure back down. But the side effects of the diuretic lingered in me for a month! I was close to my next three-month checkup and labs, and I knew my A1C would be noticeably different at that time. Mine have consistently been in the 6s, and I knew I was ready to get into trouble! Thankfully, my doctor knew what had been going on, so she was lenient when she shared my 7.4 A1C with me. She could tell, though, that I had done a good job of adjusting and pulling myself out of a rough spot. By looking at my glucometer readings, she could see the upswing in my sugar and then the downswing as I was adjusting. She actually told me that she was very impressed by the way I had adjusted to the problem.

My point in telling you this is this: You are in control, and you have to learn your own body. You have to know how you feel, and you need to take note when something is causing you to feel different. You have to check your sugars, as well, to know what is causing you to feel the way you do. I will reiterate what all the doctors will tell you, that you can't tell what your blood sugar is by how you feel. I totally agree! But I will tell you this little story to make my point.

When my kids were young and we would all be in the car or maybe at a restaurant and it was time for me to check my sugar, I would put my test strip in and put my blood on it. My daughter Shelby would grab the meter away from me or Linda. She would tell me to guess what my sugar was, and to her amazement, I would be very, very close most of the time! I would even freak her out sometimes, because I would guess it exactly.

But even though I had a good idea of how I felt and what my sugar would be, I still was checking it—just to be sure. With the arrival of continuous glucose monitors, it is really a no-brainer that you know at all times what your sugar readings are. That is an amazing advancement that has been made by the constant research being done, along with the technological advancements in our day and age. This research, and the advancements that go along with it, is why I am proud to say that for every purchase of this book, I will donate a portion of that profit to the JDRF. This is my time to do what I can to tell not just my own story, but the stories of millions of people around the world.

There are around 40,000 people in the United States diagnosed with Type 1 each year, and it is expected that by the year 2050, over 5 million people will be living with this disease. We *can* make a difference. Will you help me share my—no, *our* story—with any and all who might read it, and encourage them?

Share it with those who might be touched enough to step up financially to help with research.

Share it with the mom and dad who are at their wits' end in dealing with a rebellious teenager whose T1 is out of control.

Share it with your friend who has been struggling to control their sugar levels and is starting to experience complications.

Share it with someone who has lost a family member to the ravages that T1 can have on the body, and let them know that their loss is not forgotten, that people are trying desperately to find a cure for Type 1 diabetes.

I share my story for my aunt Rita, who never got to see me play ball, never got to see me get married, never got to see my children. She was taken from us way too soon—but I refuse to accept the same fate!

Linda and I are about to be grandparents for the first time in June 2018. Our son, Craig, and his wife, Samantha, are going to have a little boy! We are all excited, and we can't wait to meet little Ryker Moore. I know that I have to do everything that I can to be there for him and for my kids. All of us in the Type 1 family need to do everything that we can to help find a cure for this disease. We need to put a stop to the worry that we all have of not being around for our grandchildren. Or the worry of knowing that there is a chance of your grandchildren developing T1 based on their genetic makeup, and the dreaded fear of them not being able to withstand the struggles of this disease and dying young.

We can put an end to this, and my prayer is that it comes quickly!

I want to thank you for reading my story. I hope that it has been an encouragement to you. I hope and pray that if you have T1, you're able to reach all of your dreams, and that you let no obstacles get in your way, especially diabetes. I hope that your parents are there for you like mine were for me.

Parents of children with T1, I hope and pray that you can love them and support them, and help them grow their wings so they can fly as high as they possibly can. Be there for them, through the good and the bad times, and they will forever love you for it.

Most importantly, I hope and pray for the day when we will live in a world without Type 1 diabetes!

DID YOU KNOW?

Living with Type 1 diabetes can be tough, but with proper care, it can be just a footnote in your life's story. Balancing nutrition, exercise, and proper blood glucose management techniques with the rest of your life's priorities means that anything is possible for you!

Left to right: Michael, Linda, and Melissa

What can I say about Michael…my partner in crime, or should I say my "leader" in crime!?

I was the last of five children, with Michael being just three years older than me. I would like to say that he got me in a lot of trouble, but technically, I might have been a bit spoiled, being the baby and all, and I whined to Mom whenever he did something to irritate me, and then Michael would endure the wrath of our mother from picking on the "baby."

Time spent following Michael around was time well spent. There was always something adventurous or mischievous around every corner. One such incident took place when someone in the family had gotten new shoes and Michael took the shoe box and turned it into a "house." He added a front door, windows, and some Magic Marker detailing to make this house quite nice, and obviously livable, because Michael decided that one of my Fisher Price Little People should inhabit it. But Michael's creative mind was already taking things to another level. Little did I know what my poor Little People boy with the ball cap was going to endure that day.

We took the shoe box house outside, along with the Little People boy. Michael said we needed to get right up next to our house so Mom couldn't see what we were doing. Uh-oh! That should have been my first clue that something was about to go wrong. But I chose to stay by Michael's side while he proceeded to concoct a "fire emergency" in the shoe box house, with my Little People tenant inside! You see, Michael had gotten a new toy fire truck that actually sprayed water, and he wanted to try it out on a "real" housefire.

I know you may be thinking that we started a fire in our own house, too, but no, something far worse took place. The fire was lit, the shoe box house was burning, my Little People boy was trapped inside the burning house—and all the while we were tucked right up against our own house for fear of getting in trouble for playing with fire.

But then…sirens started blaring out of Michael's mouth as his new water-spraying fire truck came roaring up to the burning house. Firefighter Michael began to successfully put out the fire in the brand-new shoe box home and rushed in to save my Little People boy! Michael pulled my little baseball cap–wearing, FAVORITE Little People right out of the fire, only to discover that the bill on his baseball cap had melted right off in the fire. He was now wearing just a beanie!

I was devastated and ohhhh, so angry! My favorite little guy was no longer a cute little baseball player! I was heartbroken over the loss.

I'm not sure if Michael ever apologized to me for burning the bill off my Little People boy's hat, but I'm pretty sure I ran to Mom and told on him, which ended up revealing that we had set a shoe box on fire right next to our own house, which got him into a lot of trouble! I got my payback!

I never realized as a kid just how much I loved my adventure-seeking brother until a few years later, when he started having some health issues. Mom took him to the doctor one Saturday morning to see what was going on. My sister and I were the only ones at home when Mom called from the doctor to tell us that Michael had been diagnosed with juvenile diabetes and was going to be admitted to the hospital. I wanted to look strong to my older sister, so I went to the bathroom where she couldn't see me, and I cried my eyes out. My heart was hurting so deeply because I did not know what the future would hold for Michael.

Michael was diagnosed with Juvenile Diabetes over thirty-nine years ago at the age of fifteen. Life dramatically changed for him at such a young age, but he has never let it slow him down or hinder him in any way. He has learned to manage the disease, and he is in great health today because he has a zest for life and wants to live it to the fullest! He is still adventurous and fun-loving, and whenever our crazy-busy adult lives allow us time together, I find myself still following him around…and there is still something adventurous, or mischievous, around every corner.

Kevin Perry

A Note from My Friend, Kevin Perry

Michael, I remember how hard you worked to learn about diabetes. You could tell us more than most doctors probably knew. You did a pretty good job of watching what you ate, but we didn't always watch what we drank. We often let our youth trump our intelligence.

I look back with such fond memories of high school bus trips to games. It is still very clear to me how you did your best to make sure that you were eating the right things and monitoring your blood sugar levels, and I still remember giving you insulin injections. It was funny how it freaked out some of our friends. Between you and my nana, I gave several injections throughout my life! It was not anything that I would have ever wished on my best friend, but I wouldn't have changed how it made our friendship even closer.

I LOVE YOU, BROTHER!!!

Made in the USA
Monee, IL
07 July 2026

56551534R00056